First World War
and Army of Occupation
War Diary
France, Belgium and Germany

40 DIVISION
119 Infantry Brigade
East Surrey Regiment
13th Battalion
1 February 1918 - 31 July 1918

WO95/2606/4

The Naval & Military Press Ltd
www.nmarchive.com
Published in association with The National Archives

Published by

The Naval & Military Press Ltd

Unit 10 Ridgewood Industrial Park,

Uckfield, East Sussex,

TN22 5QE England

Tel: +44 (0) 1825 749494

www.naval-military-press.com

www.nmarchive.com

This diary has been reprinted in facsimile from the original. Any imperfections are inevitably reproduced and the quality may fall short of modern type and cartographic standards.

© **Crown Copyright**
Images reproduced by permission of The National Archives, London, England, 2015.

Contents

Document type	Place/Title	Date From	Date To
Heading	WO95/2606/4 13 Battalion East Surrey Regiment		
Heading	40th Division 119th Infy Bde 13th Bn East Surrey Regt Feb 1918-Jly 1918 From 120 Bde To U K 1918 July		
Heading	War Diary for the month of February 1918 13th Bn East Surrey Regt. 119th Infantry Brigade 40th Division Volume 21.		
War Diary	No 8 Camp Mory.	01/02/1918	02/02/1918
War Diary	No 8 Camp Mory and Left Sub-Sector Noreuil	03/02/1918	04/02/1918
War Diary	Left Sub-Sector Norevil.	05/02/1918	09/02/1918
War Diary	Left Sub-Sector Norevil and Armagh Camp.	10/02/1918	10/02/1918
War Diary	Armagh Camp and No 3 Camp Hendecourt.	11/02/1918	12/02/1918
War Diary	No 8 Camp Hendecourt	13/02/1918	16/02/1918
War Diary	No 8 Camp Hendecourt York Lines.	17/02/1918	20/02/1918
War Diary	York Lines and No. 3 Camp Hendecourt.	21/02/1918	21/02/1918
War Diary	No 3 Camp Hendecourt.	22/02/1918	27/02/1918
War Diary	No 3 Camp Hendecourt and Monchiet.	28/02/1918	28/02/1918
Heading	40th Division. 119th Infantry Brigade. 13th Battalion. East Surrey Regiment March 1918.		
Heading	13th (S) Bn East Surrey Regt. War Diary Volume No March-1918 Vol 22.		
Miscellaneous			
War Diary	Monchiet.	01/03/1918	02/03/1918
War Diary	Monchiet & No. 3 Camp Hendecourt.	03/03/1918	03/03/1918
War Diary	Hendecourt.	04/03/1918	11/03/1918
War Diary	Hendecourt To Carlisle Camp Merchtel.	12/03/1918	12/03/1918
War Diary	Mercatel.	13/03/1918	17/03/1918
War Diary	Carlisle Camp.	18/03/1918	21/03/1918
War Diary	Rendezvous Near St Judas Farm St Leger.	22/03/1918	22/03/1918
War Diary	Ervillers	23/03/1918	26/03/1918
War Diary	Wood.	26/03/1918	26/03/1918
War Diary	Sombrin To Houvelin.	29/03/1918	29/03/1918
War Diary	Houvelin.	30/03/1918	30/03/1918
War Diary	Ervillers.	24/03/1918	26/03/1918
War Diary	Ervillers To Bucquoy.	27/03/1918	27/03/1918
War Diary	In Support Trenches Near Adinfer Wood.	28/03/1918	28/03/1918
War Diary	Sombrin To Houvelin.	29/03/1918	29/03/1918
War Diary	Houvelin.	30/03/1918	31/03/1918
Miscellaneous	Headquarters. 119th Infantry Brigade.		
Miscellaneous	13 E Surrey Honours & Awards.		
Heading	40th Division. 119th Infantry Brigade 13th Battalion The East Surrey Regiment April 1918.		
Heading	13th (S) Bn. East Surrey Regt. War Diary Volume No. 23 April 1918.		
Miscellaneous			
War Diary	Houvelin & Neuf Berquin.	01/04/1918	01/04/1918
War Diary	Nouveau Monde.	02/04/1918	30/04/1918
Heading	13th (S) Bn East Surrey Regt. War Diary Volume No. 24 May 1918.		
Miscellaneous			
War Diary	Nieurlet Oudezeele.	01/05/1918	01/05/1918

War Diary	Nieurlet.	02/05/1918	06/05/1918
War Diary	Booninghem.	07/05/1918	10/05/1918
War Diary	Queue D'Oxelaere.	11/05/1918	18/05/1918
War Diary	La Belle Hotesse.	18/05/1918	29/05/1918
War Diary	Les Trois Rois.	30/05/1918	31/05/1918
Heading	13th (S) Bn East Surrey Regt. War Diary Volume No. 25 June 1918.		
Miscellaneous			
War Diary	Les Trois Rois.	01/06/1918	02/06/1918
War Diary	Hardinghen.	03/06/1918	10/06/1918
War Diary	Bayenghem.	11/06/1918	30/06/1918
Heading	13th (S) Bn East Surrey Regt. War Diary Volume No. July 1918.		
War Diary	Mytchett Camp Aldershot	01/07/1918	09/07/1918
War Diary	Aldershot.	10/07/1918	16/07/1918
War Diary	Lowestoft.	17/07/1918	21/07/1918
War Diary	Lowestoft	22/07/1918	31/07/1918

WO95/2606/4
13 Battalion East Surrey Regiment

40TH DIVISION
119TH INFY BDE

13TH BN EAST SURREY REGT

FEB 1918-JLY 1918

From 120 Bde

To UK 1918 JLY

WAR DIARY
or
INTELLIGENCE SUMMARY.

WAR DIARY

for the month of

FEBRUARY 1918.

13th Bn East Surrey Regt

119th INFANTRY BRIGADE

40th DIVISION

VOLUME 21.

WAR DIARY or INTELLIGENCE SUMMARY

Army Form C. 2118.

13TH Bn EAST SURREY REGT   119th BRIGADE   40 DIVISION

Place	Date	Hour	Summary of Events and Information	Remarks and references to Appendices
No 8 Camp MORY	1/2/18		Trenches dug around huts by Companies. Demonstration in Guard Mounting, Saluting, Bayonet fighting & by Brigade Demonstration Platoon.	Appx 57c 28/1/2
	2/2/18		Parades under Company Commanders, ragging continued. Trench foot baths at MORY were allotted to the Battalion.	Nil of y
No 8 Camp MORY and left sub-sector NOREUIL	3/2/18		The Battalion relieved the 11th Kings Own Royal Lancs Rgt in the left sub-sector NOREUIL. Relief complete by 8.30 pm. Patrols were sent out by night and left Companies - Enemy was very quiet. LIEUT-COL H.I. WARDEN, D.S.O. left the Bttn to temporarily take command of 120 Inf Batt MAJOR INGPEN temporarily took over command of the Bn.	MGT HENDERSCOURT Nil. 120 Inf Bttn of the Bn
	4/2/18		Usual work in progress. Our Artillery fired on enemy trenches BUNNY HUG LANE and SELBY LANE. Enemy shelled TANK AVENUE and RAILWAY RESERVE with 77mm and 105 mm. Patrols went out throughout the night. Hostile MG located at U29 a 8.7.	Nil.

WAR DIARY or INTELLIGENCE SUMMARY

Army Form C. 2118.

13TH EAST SURREY REGT
119 INF BDE
40 DIVISION

Place	Date	Hour	Summary of Events and Information	Remarks and references to Appendices
Left out-posts NOREUIL	5/2/18		Usual work in progress TANK AVENUE and RAILWAY RESERVE shelled with 77mm Patrols examined sunken road U29 a 50.65 and found it clear of enemy. LIEUT CROWTHER returned to Brigade.	MAP U29 a 50.65
	6/2/18		Our artillery fired on back areas HERMIES and NOREUIL Machine Guns fired on LONDON SUPPORT and PUDSEY SUPPORT Much movement on HENDECOURT – RIENCOURT ROAD. Enemy answered from Rifle and L/G companies. LIEUT SIMPSON returned from leave	
	7/2/18	6.30am	Our M.G's fired an SOS line to Enemy had made an attempt upon the OP but was not ruled but barrage came up & nothing along the front. Artillery on both sides kept busy throughout the day. 2/LIEUT W.E. DOBB and wounded (accepted) Reinforcements:- 2/LIEUT E. JORDAN RLT BATTERY 2/LT F. SIMMONDS 2/ 11TH ROYAL 2/LT H.J. SMITH MGC. BROR from 7th Bn EAST SURREY REGT	

WAR DIARY
or
INTELLIGENCE SUMMARY

13TH BN EAST SURREY REGT.
Army Diaries and Intelligence / 119 INF BDE / 40 DIVISION.

Army Form C. 2118.

Place	Date	Hour	Summary of Events and Information	Remarks and references to Appendices
In Sub Sect. MOEUVRES	8/2/18		18 strenuous men W/S hour shelled HERMIES COURT during the day. Enemy shelled TANK AVENUE with 77mm. Enemy patrols were sent out throughout the hours of darkness. Usual work. LIEUT A.C. THOMPSON proceeded to England for branch duty.	WAR HERMIES COURT. Mr.
	9/2/18		One auxiliary funnel saw BUNNY HUG at O29 a 75 80. Heavy french mortar. We fired on SELBY LANE. Patrols were sent out from night and Regt. Conferences. Work on trenches in progress. 2/LIEUT W.B. PARKER proceeded on leave. LIEUT R.R. WEBB. 2/LIEUT. H.E. BEATON Reinforcements "Lieut H BUCK from 7th BN EAST SURREY REGT.	Mrs.
Left sub sect	10/2/18		The Battn was relieved by 2/6th NORTH STAFFORDSHIRE REGT. (less 1 Coy + 2 platoons). Right front Coy A] relieved by D Coy 2/6 NORTH STAFFS REGT Left front Coy C] "" Right support Coy D] relieved by C Coy (plus 2 plns) -do- Left support B] "" The Battalion proceeded from SUGAR FACTORY by bus to ARMAGH CAMP. 2/Lt F.J. CHITTY was admitted to hospital from 40 DIVNL SIGNAL SCHOOL 2/Lt E.J. WILKS joined the Battn from 7TH EAST SURREY REGT	

MOEUVRES and ARMAGH CAMP

Army Form C. 2118.

13TH BN EAST SURREY REGT.
119 INF BDE
40 DIVN

WAR DIARY
or
INTELLIGENCE SUMMARY.
(Erase heading not required.)

Instructions regarding War Diaries and Intelligence Summaries are contained in F. S. Regs., Part II. and the Staff Manual respectively. Title pages will be prepared in manuscript.

Place	Date	Hour	Summary of Events and Information	Remarks and references to Appendices
ARMAGH CAMP and N.S. CAMP HENDECOURT	18/5/18		Bn and Artillery moved by lorries at 200 yards interval to No.3 CAMP HENDECOURT via BOISLEUX AU MONT and RICHEUX. Arriving at 1pm	
		2pm to 11pm	Coys & Companies reached with feet inspections and general cleaning up.	
	19/5/18		Several minor bombing tournaments — kit inspections sent Coy Reports Staff Drill inspection. CAPT F S HAYDEN returned from leave and taken on duty as adjutant. LT CORBETT and LT SMITH returned from leave. MAJOR L. FRASER on duty from 7th EAST SURREY REGT. POSTING: The draft of officers and 192 OR from 7th EAST SURREY REGT. was posted as follows:—	
			MAJOR LT TR WEBB B COY Y2E T R DAN A COY TO 7TH EAST SURREY REGT	
			}{ H BRIEN GY TARRY AT WULKA WE BELINA	
			A/CH & STANDFORDS	
			F CH	
	20/5/18		The Major General congratulates all ranks in the Brigade for the amount of work done & by the Brigade in ... the period the Brigade was in the line	

Army Form C. 2118.

WAR DIARY or INTELLIGENCE SUMMARY.

(Erase heading not required.)

13TH BN EAST SURREY REGT
Instructions regarding War Diaries and Intelligence 119 BDE
Summaries are contained in F. S. Regs., Part II.
and the Staff Manual respectively. Title pages 40 DIVISION.
will be prepared in manuscript.

Place	Date	Hour	Summary of Events and Information	Remarks and references to Appendices
#7 No 3 Camp Morbecque	12/2/18		Parade under Company Commanders. Platoon and Company drill. Also Reports Appx 87³ drill to be held at BLARINGHIE. Visited the Baths. All new joined N.C.O.s were inspected by the Medical Officer. The officers who dined in M.O.'s.	
	14/2/18	10.30	Parade under Company Commanders. Platoon drill. Company Commanders drill to the sub.	
		1-3pm	Musketry	
		6-8.30pm 9-2.30pm	Miniature Range XIIa allotted to A Coy. under supervision of Musketry Officer.	
			ALSO LIEUT. J.E.M. MICHELMORE attached MUSKETRY OFFR	
			LIEUT F. SIMPSON] LEWIS GUN OFFR	
			LT R.H.T. PEACOCK rejoined the Bn from leave	
			2/LIEUT MUKENCAMP evacuated to England – Sick	
	15/2/18		Parades under Coy Commanders – Platoon and Company drill 10-12.	
		9-12.30pm 2-3pm	Musketry Miniature Range XIIa allotted to B Coy	
		2pm	The Battn. was transferred to 119 Infantry Brigade in place of 10/11 Highland Light Infantry.	
	16/2/18		Parades under Company Commanders. Company drill. Coy drill & Musketry. Miniature Range XIIb allotted to C Coy under supervision of Musketry Officer and refits of Battn inspected by Brigadier Armouries. Lecture on intelligence at Divl. Bonfrey. At MONT attended by 22 officers 26 OR Capt R.B. BURTON Capt R.W.H. KING. LIEUT J.E.M. CROWTHER proceeded on leave to England. LT HEAD arrived 13rd from lv. course to England.	

A584 Wt. W4973 M687 730,000 8/16 D. D. & L. Ltd. Forms/C.2118/13.

WAR DIARY or INTELLIGENCE SUMMARY

Army Form C. 2118.

13th Bn EAST SURREY REGT.
119 BRIGADE. 40 DIVISION.

Place	Date	Hour	Summary of Events and Information	Remarks and references to Appendices
BEAUCOURT YORK LINES	17/2/18	10 am	The Battn moved by Companies at 200 yards intervals to YORK LINES MERCATEL taking over the Camp from 10/11 Highland Light Infantry	map 57c
	18/2/18		Parade under Company Commanders — Company Drill & Range practice fired by C Company under supervision of Musketry Officer. Duty for Piquet Officer 1 NCO and 20 men detailed	
	19/2/18	12:30	Company & Platoon Commanders Drill. Lectures on Message Carrying given to Officers and men and arrangements for Coops Pigeon Officer Lt H. ANDREW attached to 40 Divl.	
	20/2/18	12:30 pm	Parades under Company Commanders Drill in CAMP and LINES were allotted to the Battalion. Transport was inspected by Divisional General Remarks favourable. Officers and N.C.O's reassembled for service to spots assembly for the event of any enemy to life for special attention notices	
FORT KNOT HENRIETTE	21/2/18	9 am 2.3/p	Battn moved by Companies at 200 yards intervals to No 3 Camp HENRIETTE marched to dinning equipment enpluse	

Army Form C. 2118.

13TH BN EAST SURREY REGT   119 BDE   40 DIVN

WAR DIARY
or
INTELLIGENCE SUMMARY.
(Erase heading not required.)

Instructions regarding War Diaries and Intelligence Summaries are contained in F.S. Regs., Part II. and the Staff Manual respectively. Title pages will be prepared in manuscript.

Place	Date	Hour	Summary of Events and Information	Remarks and references to Appendices
No 3 Camp HENDECOURT	22/9/18	9-1pm	Battalion inspection by Commanding Officer	Appx 57c
		2-3	Parades under Company Commanders and Specialists	
	23/9/18	9-1pm	Inspection of the Brigade by General Officer Commanding	Appx 7
		2-4pm	Sports	
			2/LIEUT. W B PARKER returned from leave	
	24/9/18	10am	Church parade	
			Areas at BLAIRVILLE were allotted to the Battn & Commanding Officer together with Company Commanders reconnoitred positions of assembly in the event of enemy attacking the left Division (Corps front)	Appx 7
			2/T COL H L WARDEN DSO assumed command of the Battalion	
	25/9/18	9-1pm	Paraded under Company Commanders	Appx
			Zero Bombers fired on miniature range	
			Pigeoneer paraded under Bn Signalling Officer	
		3.30pm	G.O.C. talked to all Officers & sgn Brigade	
		4pm	G.O.C. lectured to all NCOs	
	26/9/18	9-12	Miniature Range — All companies	Appx
		4pm	Recce practice — all Officers	

A5834 Wt. W4973/M687 750,000 8/16 D. D. & L. Ltd. Forms/C.2118/13.

Army Form C. 2118.

WAR DIARY or INTELLIGENCE SUMMARY

13th BN EAST SURREY REGT 119 BRIGADE 40 DIVN.

Instructions regarding War Diaries and Intelligence Summaries are contained in F.S. Regs., Part II. and the Staff Manual respectively. Title pages will be prepared in manuscript.

(Erase heading not required.)

Place	Date	Hour	Summary of Events and Information	Remarks and references to Appendices
No 3 Camp HEDDEQUE	20/1/18	(cont)	Men on potato fatigue employed for by HQ 119 Bde. Distribution of Motor Rota Ref 52 Ref to Intelligence Section lined :- 1 Officer 1 Sgt 1/1/18 18 OR. By HQ Intelligence officer from 2nd Bn. 1 For Release HP. CAPT O.G. HERMAN having rejoined the Bn. in duty was posted to C Company as 2nd in command of that company.	
			Appointments:-	
			Tn Signalling Offr 2nd Lt. F R WOODWARD	
			Intelligence - F S BISHOP	
			Lewis Gun - Lt F SIMONDS	
			Musketry Offr Lt J.E.M. MIDDLEMORE	
			Bombing 2nd Lt H.S SMITH	
	21/1/18	9am	Inspections made by Commander Nature and pay for 18th	
		9 "	Operations order and Signal Officer	
		2-5pm	Musketry Ranges X HA and XHA visited by all Coy Musketry Officers	
			Musketry Officer	
		9.30am	All rifles Lewis guns and Lewis buckets inspected by Armourer	
			Armourer Sergeant	
			Battalion Stats	
		3pm	Lt HUGHES proceeded to England on 14 days duty	

Army Form C. 2118.

WAR DIARY
or
INTELLIGENCE SUMMARY.

13th Bn EAST SURREY REGT.
119 Bde
110 Divn

(Erase heading not required.)

Place	Date	Hour	Summary of Events and Information	Remarks and references to Appendices
HENDECOURT	28/3/18		On Battalion proceeded to MONCHIET via ADDINFER - RANSART - BEAU METZ. Companies at 100 yards interval. Arrived 1.30pm	Map Sheet
MONCHIET			CASUALTIES. Wounded — 1 Officer 4 O.R.	Mk.

H. Warden Lieut. Col.
Commdg 13th Bn East Surrey Rgt

40th Division.
119th Infantry Brigade.

WAR DIARY

13th BATTALION

EAST SURREY REGIMENT

MARCH 1918

13TH (S) BN EAST SURREY REGT.

WAR DIARY.

VOLUME No

MARCH — 1918.

CONFIDENTIAL.

Army Form C. 2118.

WAR DIARY
or
INTELLIGENCE SUMMARY.

(Erase heading not required.)

Instructions regarding War Diaries and Intelligence Summaries are contained in F. S. Regs., Part II. and the Staff Manual respectively. Title pages will be prepared in manuscript.

Place	Date	Hour	Summary of Events and Information	Remarks and references to Appendices

(A2-04) D. D. & L., London, E.C. Wt. W.77/M2031 750,000 5/19 Sch. 52 Forms/C2116/14

Army Form C. 2118.

WAR DIARY
or
INTELLIGENCE SUMMARY.

13th (S) Bn. East Surrey Regt.
119th Infantry Brigade.
40th Division.

(Erase heading not required.)

Instructions regarding War Diaries and Intelligence Summaries are contained in F. S. Regs., Part II. and the Staff Manual respectively. Title pages will be prepared in manuscript.

Place	Date	Hour	Summary of Events and Information	Remarks and references to Appendices
MONCHIET	1/3/18	9.45 A.M.	Brigade Route March - MONCHIET - BEAUMETZ - BERNEVILLE - WARLUS - WANQUETIN - HAUTEVILLE - FOSSEUX - GUOY - MONCHIET.	MAP: LENS 13. 11.
MONCHIET	2/3/18	10 A.M.	Battalion Route March - BASSEUX - BAILLEUVAL - BAILLEULVAL MONT - MONCHIET. Afternoon devoted to Sports.	
MONCHIET AND CAMP	3/3/18	10.30 A.M.	Brigade moved to BLAIREVILLE AREA. Battalion to No. 3 Camp, HENDECOURT. Route - BEAUMETZ - RIVIERE - BRETENCOURT - BLAIREVILLE.	
HENDECOURT	4/3/18	8.30 A.M. 12.30 P.M. 1.30 P.M. 3 P.M.	Parades carried out under Company arrangements.	
HENDECOURT	5/3/18	8.30 A.M. 12 M.N. 10 A.M. to 12.30 P.M. 1.30 P.M. 3 P.M.	Preparation for Battalion Manoeuvres. Battalion Manoeuvres: Practice attack carried out in the region of X.5. Parades carried out under Company arrangements. Capt. R.W.H.King ("A" Coy), Capt.A.B.Burton ("C" Coy) and Lieut.J.E.M.Crowther ("B" Coy) reported back from leave to the United Kingdom.	* SHEET 57° S.E.
HENDECOURT	6/3/18	8.30 A.M. to 12.15 P.M. 4 P.M. to 5 P.M.	Brigade manoeuvres: Brigade in the attack, carried out in the region of X.5. Enemy and Barrage were imaginary. The afternoon was devoted to sport. Lecture delivered in Theatre, BLAIREVILLE, by Sir George Paish on "The effect of the War on the World's wealth".	

Army Form C. 2118.

WAR DIARY
or
INTELLIGENCE SUMMARY.
(Erase heading not required.)

Instructions regarding War Diaries and Intelligence Summaries are contained in F. S. Regs., Part II. and the Staff Manual respectively. Title pages will be prepared in manuscript.

Place	Date	Hour	Summary of Events and Information	Remarks and references to Appendices
HENDECOURT	7/3/18	9.30 a.m. to 1.15 p.m. 2 p.m. to 3 p.m.	Brigade manoeuvres (Brigade in the attack) carried out on the same ground as the preceding day.. There was a flagged barrage and the enemy consisted of the T.M.B. Parades under Company arrangements.	5/4/19
HENDECOURT	8/3/18	9.30 a.m. to 12.30 p.m. 1.30 p.m. to 3 p.m. 6 p.m. to 7 p.m.	Battalion and Brigade inspection by Corps Commander. Parades under Company arrangements. Lecture by an Officer of 12th Squadron R.F.C., on "Co-operation of R.F.C. and Infantry" in the Theatre, BLAIREVILLE.	5/4/19
HENDECOURT	9/3/18	8.30 a.m. to 12.30 p.m.	Battalion manoeuvres. Battalion in the attack. Afternoon devoted to sport.	5/4/19
HENDECOURT	10/3/18	10 a.m. 6.30 p.m.	Church Parade on Camp Square. Concert in Theatre, BLAIREVILLE, by Battalion Concert Party.	5/4/19
HENDECOURT	11/3/18	8.30 a.m. to 12.30 p.m. 11.30 a.m. to 12.30 p.m. 1.30 p.m. to 3 p.m.	Battalion manoeuvres. Battalion in the attack. Battalion drill. Parades under Company arrangements.	5/4/19
HENDECOURT TO CARLISLE CAMP, MERCATEL	12/3/18		Battalion moved to CARLISLE CAMP arriving 7.30 p.m. Details left at No. 3 Camp, HENDECOURT. Battalion under orders to move at 1 hour's notice.	5/4/19
MERCATEL	13/3/18		Battalion engaged in Musketry training under Company arrangements. Specialist training under Specialist Officers. Battalion under orders to move at 1 hour's notice at night and 3 hours in day time. (8 a.m. - 8 p.m.) Parades - 8.30 a.m. - 3.30 p.m.	5/4/19

Army Form C. 2118.

WAR DIARY
or
INTELLIGENCE SUMMARY.

(Erase heading not required.)

Instructions regarding War Diaries and Intelligence Summaries are contained in F. S. Regs., Part II. and the Staff Manual respectively. Title pages will be prepared in manuscript.

Place	Date	Hour	Summary of Events and Information	Remarks and references to Appendices
MERCATEL	14/3/18	8.30 AM TO 3.30 PM	Battalion engaged in Musketry. Kit inspections: all deficiencies to be replaced. Battalion under orders to move at 1 hour's notice at night and 3 hours in day time.	A.W.R
MERCATEL	15/3/18	8.30 AM TO 3 PM	Battalion training - extended order drill - box respirator drill - under Company arrangements. "Hun Prepare" message came through. (Test) Specialist Classes under Specialist Officers.	A.W.R
MERCATEL	16/3/18	8.30 AM TO 3 PM	Parades under Company arrangements - extended order drill - bayonet fighting, Etc. Specialist training under Specialist Officers. Inspection of Lewis gunners by G.O.C. 119th Infantry Brigade.	A.W.R
MERCATEL	17/3/18	10.30 AM 7.30 PM	Divine Services in the morning. Working party of 335 Other Ranks, supplied by the Battalion to work in the NEUVILLE VITASSE area commencing 7.30 p.m.	A.W.R
CARLISLE CAMP	18/3/18		Parades 8.30 a.m. - 12.30 p.m. Extended order drill; practice attack on Strong points. Tank demonstration at WAILLY 10.30 a.m. Working party of 500 all ranks parading 6.45 p.m. Lieut. G. E. Deacon proceeded on special leave to England.	A.W.R
CARLISLE CAMP	19/3/18		Parades 10.30 a.m. - 12.30 p.m. Practice of Battalion in attack on a succession of Strong points. Parades 1.30 p.m. - 3 p.m. Specialists under Special Officers. Working party of 250 under Major W.G. West.	A.W.R

Army Form C. 2118.

WAR DIARY
or
INTELLIGENCE SUMMARY.
(Erase heading not required.)

Instructions regarding War Diaries and Intelligence Summaries are contained in F. S. Regs., Part II. and the Staff Manual respectively. Title pages will be prepared in manuscript.

Place	Date	Hour	Summary of Events and Information	Remarks and references to Appendices
CARLISLE CAMP	20/3/18		Parades. Tank demonstration at WAILLY 10.30 a.m. with an exercise in tactics carried out by "D" Coy. All available Officers and N.C.Os of A, B, and C Coys parades at 7.20 a.m. and proceeded to WAILLY. Other ranks paraded at 8.30 a.m. - 12.30 p.m. and continued construction of sod barricades to protect NISSEN Huts in Camp. Working party under Capt. O. G. Norman of 250 O.Rs. 1.30 p.m. - 3 p.m. Specialists under Specialist Officers.	
CARLISLE CAMP	21/3/18		Hostile bombardment on Corps Front commencing 5 a.m. and continuing all morning. Battalion in readiness to move. All parades cancelled by order G.O.C. and men resting. Battalion under orders to move at half-an-hour's notice. Bombardment somewhat abated in the afternoon. Little aerial activity on the part of the enemy in the immediate vicinity of the Camp. Battalion moved off at half-an-hour's notice at 4.15 p.m. but this move was countermanded. Battalion moved off to HENIN at 5 p.m. and subsequently on reaching HENIN (11.30 p.m.) Battalion then marched on to	
RENDEZVOUS NEAR ST JUDAS FARM. ST LEGER.	22/3/18		Dug-outs on the HENIN-CROISELLES ROAD where the Battalion dug itself in till 2.30 a.m. Subsequently marched to a rendezvous near St. Judas Farm arriving there at 7 a.m. Heavy hostile bombardment by the enemy who it appeared had attacked on a 60 miles front and, having captured CROISILLES, were advancing supported by their batteries against us. Bombardment lasted all day. "D" Coy ordered into front line near ST. LEGER at 2 p.m. Slight aerial activity.	
ERVILLERS	23/3/18		Marched (starting at 5.30 a.m.) to ERVILLERS, and attack on MORY by "B" Coy, and later supported by "C" and "D" Coys at 2.30 p.m. Casualties to Officers: Capt. O. G. Norman (wounded), Lieut. W.V.L.Mallett (killed) Lieut. J.E.M. Crowther (wounded) 2/Lieuts. G.R.Tarry, F.A.Simmonds, H.M.S.Bailey, E.Skidmore wounded in attacking enemy position on MORY RIDGE.	

Army Form C. 2118.

WAR DIARY
or
INTELLIGENCE SUMMARY.

(Erase heading not required.)

Instructions regarding War Diaries and Intelligence Summaries are contained in F. S. Regs., Part II. and the Staff Manual respectively. Title pages will be prepared in manuscript.

Place	Date	Hour	Summary of Events and Information	Remarks and references to Appendices
ERVILLERS	24/3/18		Lieut. A.G.J.Altman wounded, the attacking Companies of the East Surrey were in a position on the right and left flank of MORY Village and were continuing to press their attack. About 10 p.m. attack by enemy stopped by our artillery, prisoners reporting heavy casualties among those attacking.	A/18
ERVILLERS	25/3/17		Capt. R.W.H.King wounded, and Lieut. D.E.Berney (U.S.R.M.C.) wounded. Enemy reported advancing in large numbers.	A/18
ERVILLERS	26/3/18		Enemy seen advancing in large numbers over crests and ridges behind MORY Village. Composite Companies of East Surreys entrenched on crest of slope overlooking MORY.	A/18
			Battalion evacuated ERVILLERS after heavy fighting, our own artillery firing short and causing casualties to us in Sunken Road near Quarry which was our Headquarters. Battalion collected from neighbouring trenches in ERVILLERS. BEHAGNIES occupied by the Germans after being evacuated by our troops. Enemy reported in considerable numbers and supported by Cavalry by Lieut. Col. Rowley: Manchesters advancing over the ridges towards MORY and ERVILLERS.	M/18
WOOD.			Battalion moving to MONCHY AU BOIS, was halted near ADINFER WOOD, and took up position at 11 a.m. near ADINFER WOOD. Germans shelling road which was heavily congested with transport and troops. Battalion remained in trenches till 3 a.m. when we received our orders to march to HARBACQ. These were countermanded on our march and we were ordered to SOMBRIN where we arrived at 11.30 a.m. and rested.	M/18
SOMBRIN TO HOUVELIN	29/3/18		Battalion marched to HOUVELIN, falling in under orders at 7.30 a.m. Lorries were to be provided for those who had fought in the line, but there was some hitch and most of the party had to march. Accommodation for 400 only.	M/18
HOUVELIN	30/3/18		Battalion strength near 800. Billets bad and cramped quarters. Day devoted to cleaning up, rest, ascertaining deficiencies of kit, baths.	A/18

The above seem at wrong... [attached note, partially illegible]

WAR DIARY
or
INTELLIGENCE SUMMARY.

(Erase heading not required.)

Army Form C. 2118.

Place	Date	Hour	Summary of Events and Information	Remarks and references to Appendices
ERVILLERS	24/3/17		Lieut. A.G.J. Altman wounded, the attacking Companies of the East Surrey were in a position on the right and left flank of MORY Village and were continuing to press their attack. About 10 p.m. attack by enemy stopped by our artillery, prisoners reporting heavy casualties among those attacking.	
ERVILLERS	26/3/17		Capt. R.W.H.King wounded, and Lieut. D.E.Berney (U.S.F.M.C.) wounded. Enemy reported advancing in large numbers.	
ERVILLERS	26/3/17		Enemy seen advancing in large numbers over crests and ridges behind MORY Village. Composite Companies of East Surreys entrenched on crest of slope overlooking MORY.	
ERVILLERS TO BUCQUOY	27/3/17		Battalion evacuated ERVILLERS after heavy fighting, our own artillery firing short and causing casualties to us in Sunken Road near Quarry which was our Headquarters. Battalion collected from neighbouring trenches in ERVILLERS. BEHAGNIES occupied by the Germans after being evacuated by our troops. Enemy reported in considerable numbers and supported by Cavalry by Lieut. Col. Rowley: Manchesters advancing over the ridges towards MORY and ERVILLERS.	
IN SUPPORT TRENCHES NEAR ADINFER WOOD.	28/3/17		Battalion moving to MONCHY AU BOIS, was halted near ADINFER WOOD, and took up position at 11 a.m. near ADINFER WOOD. Germans shelling road which was heavily congested with transport and troops. Battalion remained in trenches till 3 a.m. when we received our orders to march to HARBACQ. These were countermanded on our march and we were ordered to SOMBRIN where we arrived at 11.30 a.m. and rested.	
SOMBRIN TO HOUVELIN	29/3/17		Battalion marched to HOUVELIN, falling in under orders at 7.30 a.m. Lorries were to be provided for those who had fought in the line, but there was some hitch and most of the party had to march. Accommodation for 400 only.	
HOUVELIN	30/3/17		Battalion strength near 800. Billets bad and cramped quarters. Day devoted to cleaning up, rest, ascertaining deficiencies of kit, baths.	

Army Form C. 2118.

WAR DIARY
or
~~INTELLIGENCE SUMMARY.~~
(Erase heading not required.)

Instructions regarding War Diaries and Intelligence Summaries are contained in F. S. Regs., Part II. and the Staff Manual respectively. Title pages will be prepared in manuscript.

Place	Date	Hour	Summary of Events and Information	Remarks and references to Appendices
HOUVELIN	23/4/16		Easter Sunday. Divine Services and rest.	MWB
			CASUALTIES FOR MONTH.	
			Officers. Other Ranks.	
			Killed 1 17	
			Wounded 9 139	
			Missing 52	
			Lieut. Colonel, Commanding 13th (Ser.) Batt. E. Surrey Regt.	

Headquarters.
119th Infantry Brigade.

Reference your No. W/694th, dated 30.3.18, I beg the honour to submit the following short report on the recent operations in so far as this Unit was concerned.:-

On 24.3.18, the Battalion moved to HENIN HILL in accordance with orders, and dug in in support to the 2nd Middlesex, 21st Div.. On 25.3.18, the Battalion withdrew from HENIN HILL in accordance with orders, and moved to R.1.b. (Sheet 57C) South of JUDAS FARM. There it occupied the army Line across the ST LEGER VALLY, and later in the day one Company was ordered up to hold HILL SWITCH which was a Support Trench to SWITCH VALLEY.

Early on the 26.3.18, orders came to evacuate the Army Line at the ance position, and as it was rumoured that ERVILLERS had .... fallen or was in danger, I was instructed to seize it at once. I was further instructed to stop the Bot on the front of the Brigade on our right. I at once seized ERVILLERS with one Company, which dug in on a suitable line for the defence of the village. As soon as that was accomplished, and as I had been informed that that 21st Middlesex would relieve me in the defence of ERVILLERS, I moved the two other Companies which I had at that time to BEHAGNIES, in order to make certain that that village was still in our hands.

Between ERVILLERS and BEHAGNIES I found several heavy guns, ammunition dumps, water carts, lorries and considerable stores all abandoned. I got into touch with the Garrison gunners, and with certain details I found round BEHAGNIES including the C.O. of the 4th Lincolns, who, at that time, was digging in his few men in front of BEHAGNIES. I had intended to support the few troops in BEHAGNIES, as that was the weak flank to ERVILLERS, but in the course of the day I was ordered to move to ERVILLERS near INNISKILLEN CAMP, and I moved my Battalion Headquarters accordingly. After reporting to Brigade the action I had taken at BEHAGNIES, I suggested that the reconnaisance of MORY which I had made (and which had been done by one of my Companies) should be followed by a counter attack on MORY itself, and I received orders to carry this out. I accordingly attacked MORY, commencing at 2.30 p.m. The danger appeared to be the number of enemy strong points on the ridge left of MORY, and my scheme for attack was to attack with one Company (a second in support) from the left of MORY, with a third Company operating on their left flank towards the northern portion of the village, they having orders to guard the left flank of the attack and subdue enemy strong points which should interfere with it. My last Company was in Reserve, and was to move on MORY from the south, and be prepared to mop up the village when it had been taken.

Shortly after the attack started, it became obvious that there were considerable enemy machine guns and snipers in the village itself, but more important still, the Army Line west of MORY and certain trenches beyond it on the ridge were very strongly held by the enemy with machine guns. I had established Battalion Battle Headquarters on the ridge overlooking MORY, and from these I observed that my left flanking Company was in great difficulties on account of the enemy strong points and the heavy machine gun fire, and that the two attacking Companies were not making sufficient progress. I accordingly ordered my Reserve Company to proceed to make a frontal attack on the village from the South, and in the hope of providing sufficient diversion to allow my main attack to proceed, or at least to clear the village, and afterwards work round and silence the enemy strong points from the right flank. After having given these orders to my Reserve Company, I resolved to proceed to the village and endeavour to push on the main attack. When I arrived there, I found that the attack had been abandoned by orders of the Senior Officer present, and that my three flanking Companies had fallen back on a line along the low part of MORY. After these had been reorganised I instructed the attack to proceed in conjunction with my Reserve Company right through the village, and gave detailed orders as to how this was to be carried out, and the renewed attack was immediately commenced.

After dark, and as no report had come back, I ordered first my Intelligence Officer and later my Adjutant to proceed to the village and clear up the situation.

It was found that large numbers of the enemy had been accounted for, but that in addition to several casualties among the attackers, several parties of my Battalion had gone amissing. Accordingly my Adjutant gave orders for the withdrawal of fighting troops, to dig in on a line south of MORY village, and every effort was made to collect stragglers and isolated men.

During the night 23/24.3.18, fighting was hot, and it was rumoured that the enemy had broken through on the right of the 21st Middlesex, but owing to the darkness, it was impossible to tell what was happening, and the information was exceedingly confusing. As, however, it was obvious that the enemy were not getting near ERVILLERS, nothing could be done until the morning. At daybreak it was found that the enemy had broken through, and had concentrated a large number of troops in the MORY valley with the object of attacking ERVILLERS, and his attack commenced shortly after dawn. The artillery was at once informed, and they fired over MORY village on the probable position of reserves. At the same time, I as senior Commanding Officer of the Brigade, at once disposed the Brigade to form a defensive flank to guard the MORY VALLEY, to deal with the attack on ERVILLERS in enfilade. This was done in consultation with the 4th Guards Brigade who supplied part of the line. The enemy attack was completely stopped by machine gun, Lewis gun and rifle fire from this defensive flank, and large numbers of the enemy were killed and certain prisoners were also taken.

The weakness of the ERVILLERS position, however, was apparent. The defensive flank was a temporary measure, and the position of the Brigade and of the Guards Brigade was absolutely untenable, and in fact dangerous if the SENATE SWITCH at ST LEGER should break, and as there were many indications of a renewed attack on ERVILLERS, I suggested the withdrawal of the Brigade to a position from which ERVILLERS could better be defended. When orders to do this had been received from Brigade, I found that events had moved very rapidly, and that the enemy had collected large numbers of troops, and was then in fact commencing a serious attack on ERVILLERS. He had brought up his artillery close behind MORY ridge, and was shelling our troops with direct observation. I accordingly ordered the 21st Middlesex, who could best be spared from the line, to withdraw to the right flank of ERVILLERS, and dig in, and ordered the 15th Welsh to follow. I placed the 13th East Surreys under the command of the Adjutant, as I had been ordered to act as Officer in charge of Advanced Brigade Headquarters on the main ERVILLERS-BOYELLES Road, and instructed him to withdraw his Battalion after the Welsh. I also informed the 13th Yorks and the Guards Brigade of what was being done, and I then assumed command of Advanced

Brigade Headquarters. I found that all telephone communications from Advanced Brigade Headquarters had been cut, and I also saw that the SENSEE SWITCH had given way, and that the enemy was rapidly advancing down the SENSEE VALLEY, as well as down the MORY VALLEY in considerable numbers. I arranged with the Guards Brigade that they would dig in south of the ERVILLERS-BOYELLES Road, and stop the advance up the ST LEGER VALLEY, as it was found impossible to dig in on the right of ERVILLERS (because by that time BEHAGNIES had fallen also GOMIECOURT). The Middlesex, Welsh and Surreys dug in in echelon behind ERVILLERS itself, so as to protect HAMLINCOURT and MOYENNEVILLE from the south. I personally reconnoitred ~~CROISILLES~~ COURCELLES and found it deserted, but it was not occupied by the enemy.

I afterwards found Brigade Headquarters at BUCQUOY, and reported to the G.O.C. whom I found at 7 a.m. in the morning. By that time the Brigade had been concentrated in BUCQUOY. The Battalion was then marched to the South West corner of ADINFER Wood, where later it occupied trenches for the night in support of the Guards.

At 3 a.m. next morning, it marched to SOMBRIN, where it remained for two nights, and on the 28th March, it moved under orders to HOUVELIN, where it remained for two days until ordered to proceed North.

Lieut-Col.
Commanding 13th Bn East Surrey Regt.

B E Barry

40th Division.
119th Infantr/y Brigade

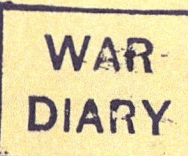

13th BATTALION

THE EAST SURREY REGIMENT

APRIL 1 9 1 8

CONFIDENTIAL

13TH (S) BN EAST SURREY REGT

WAR DIARY
VOLUME No.
APRIL 1918

Army Form C. 2118.

WAR DIARY
or
INTELLIGENCE SUMMARY.

(Erase heading not required.)

Instructions regarding War Diaries and Intelligence Summaries are contained in F. S. Regs., Part II. and the Staff Manual respectively. Title pages will be prepared in manuscript.

Place	Date	Hour	Summary of Events and Information	Remarks and references to Appendices

Army Form C. 2118.

WAR DIARY
or
INTELLIGENCE SUMMARY.
(Erase heading not required.)

Instructions regarding War Diaries and Intelligence Summaries are contained in F.S. Regs, Part II. and the Staff Manual respectively. Title pages will be prepared in manuscript.

Place	Date	Hour	Summary of Events and Information	Remarks and references to Appendices
HOUVELIN & NEUF BERQUIN	1/4/18		The Battalion, less Transport, moved to DOULIEU area. All dismounted personnel marched to BARLIN, thence by Light Railway to NEUF BERQUIN. Transport moved in Brigade group to LILLERS.	LEWIS HARTE OUT
NOUVEAU MONDE	2/4/18		Battalion marched to billets at NOUVEAU MONDE in Divisional Reserve. The Transport was brigaded at TROU BAYARD.	
	3/4/18		Parades under Company arrangements. Specialists under Specialist Officers. Box Respirator drill was included in the training.	
	4/4/18		Baths at SAILLY were allotted to the Battalion. Parades under Company arrangements. The Commanding Officer, Second-in-Command, and Company Commanders reconnoitred Strong Points in the LAVANTIE area.	
	5/4/18		Parades under Company arrangements. Specialists under Specialist Officers.	
	6/4/18		The Battalion relieved the 14th Highland Light Infantry in the Left Subsector, La Fleurbaix Sector. Right Front Coy, "A" Coy. Left Front Coy, "C" Coy. " Support " "D" " " Support " "B" " Relief was complete by 12 midnight. Lieut.Col. H.I. WARDEN admitted to hospital	
	7/4/18		Usual work on trenches in progress. Occasional gas shelling on batteries in back areas. 55 Reinforcements joined the Battalion.	
	8/4/18		Usual work in progress. Occasional gas shelling on batteries. Enemy was exceptionally quiet.	
	9/4/18		At 4.15 a.m. enemy opened intense bomb ardment on our Front and Support line. He also heavily shelled back areas. The Battalion immediately "stood to" but the enemy broke through the Portuguese on our Right flank, and the Battalion was surrounded. The men who fought their way out formed a line on the south side of the river LYS, and later took up a position in a Reserve line at LA PETIT MORTIER coming under the command of Lieut. Col. W.E.Brown, M.C.	

Army Form C. 2118.

WAR DIARY
or
INTELLIGENCE SUMMARY.

(Erase heading not required.)

Place	Date	Hour	Summary of Events and Information	Remarks and references to Appendices
	9/11/16		18th (S) Bn. Welsh Regiment. At 9 a.m. Q.M.Stores moved with Details from NOUVEAU MONDE and joined Transport at TROU BAYARD. At mid-day Headquarters of Brigade Transport was established at DOULIEU, and subsequently at NEUF BERQUIN. This place was heavily bombarded and at 5 p.m. Transport moved to LA COURANNE at which place all available men in Details (numbering 150) left to join the Battalion under 2/Lieuts. C.F.Wilks and R.H.Rowland.	

Casualties.
Killed.
Wounded.
Missing.

Officers.
Capt. G. Beaumont.
2/Lt. A. C. Cowlin.
Major W. G.West,
Capt. & Adjt. F.S.Ainger.
Capt. W. G. Price.
Capt. C. E. Linge.
Capt. A. B. Burton. (14th H.L.I.)
Lieut. R R. Webb.
Lieut. L W. Pinnick.
Lieut. J. E.M.Michelmore.
Lieut. R .H.T.Peacock.
Lieut. H W.Allason.
Lieut. W A.Morris.
Lieut. F.Pedrick. (Medical Officer)
2/Lieut. H.Buck.
2/ " c F. Jordan.
2/ " " W. B.Parker.
2/ " " J. A.V.Cant.
2/ " " H. J.Smith.
2/ " " H. E.Blatch.

Other Ranks.
7
30
437.

Killed
Wounded
Missing

Lieut. H Simonis admitted to Hospital.

Army Form C. 2118.

WAR DIARY
or
INTELLIGENCE SUMMARY.
(Erase heading not required.)

Instructions regarding War Diaries and Intelligence Summaries are contained in F. S. Regs., Part II. and the Staff Manual respectively. Title pages will be prepared in manuscript.

Place	Date	Hour	Summary of Events and Information	Remarks and references to Appendices
	10/4/18		The draft, under 2/Lieut. C.F.Wilks, joined the Battalion at LE PETIT MORTIER At noon the Battalion moved forward and occupied STEENWERCK SWITCH but was forced to retire to LA VERRIER which they occupied that night.	
	11/4/18		During the morning the Battalion to ok up a line across the Railway at LA VERRIER. The enemy made three attacks to occupy this line but was driven off each time. At 7.30 p.m. the 31st Division counter-attacked through our men who were then withdrawn. At 11 a.m. the Transport moved to Pt. Sec BOIS and at 9.30 p.m. to WALLON CAPELLE where the night was spent.	
	12/4/18		Brigade assembled at STRAZELLE and in the afternoon dug in in front of the Village. Transport moved forward to HONDEGHEM there they remained the night.	
	13/4/18		The Battalion remained in position in front of STRAZELLE until 3 p.m. when they were relieved. The Battalion then joined Transport at HONDEGHEM and, after a hot meal, marched to billets at XXXXXXX. STAPLE.	
	14/4/18		The Brigade marched via ARQUES and ST. OMER to billets at TILQUES. Lieut. Col. H.L.Warden joined the Battalion from Hospital. V " R.B.BISHOP	
	15/4/18		The Battalion moved to billets at M OULLE.	
	16/4/18		Range practices under instructors from Fourth Army School. Kit inspections. At 5.30 p.m. lecture by the Commanding Officer.	
	17/4/18		Range practices.	
	18/4/18		2 Companies sent to No. 1 Composite Brigade, attached 12th Bn. Suffolk Regiment. Lieut. G.E.Deacon proceeded to 3rd E chelon, Base.	

Army Form C. 2118.

WAR DIARY
or
INTELLIGENCE SUMMARY.
(Erase heading not required.)

Instructions regarding War Diaries and Intelligence Summaries are contained in F. S. Regs., Part II. and the Staff Manual respectively. Title pages will be prepared in manuscript.

Place	Date	Hour	Summary of Events and Information	Remarks and references to Appendices
	19/4/18		Spent clearing up records. 1 Company returned from 12th Bn. Suffolk Regiment.	
	20/4/18		Company (returned from 12th Bn. Suffolk Regt) sent to 12th Bn. Yorkshire Regiment.	
	21/4/18		Brigade moved to BOISDENGHEM via MORRINGHEM.	
	22-25/4/18		Clearing up Stores and Records. 22/4/18. 2/Lieut. O.P.Oakes to Field Ambulance.	
	26/4/18		Companies rejoined Battalion from No. 1 Composite Brigade and were billeted at LA WATTINE.	
	27/4/18		Parades under Company arrangements. Lewis gun training.	
	28/4/18		Parades under Company arrangements. Gas drill. Lewis gun training, etc.	
	29/4/18		Baths at NORTBECOURT were allotted the Battalion. Remainder of the day spent in Lewis Gun training.	
	30/4/18		Brigade moved to NIEURLET. The Commanding Officer, Adjutant, and Company Commanders reconnoitred the Army Line E. of POPERINGHE.	

H. Borden
Lieut. Colonel,
Commanding 13th (Ser.) Batt. Surrey Regt.

CONFIDENTIAL

Vol 24

24 D
6 sheets

13TH (S) BN EAST SURREY REGT.

WAR DIARY.

VOLUME No

MAY 1918.

Army Form C. 2118.

WAR DIARY
or
INTELLIGENCE SUMMARY.

(Erase heading not required.)

WAR DIARY

NOVEMBER

1918

Instructions regarding War Diaries and Intelligence
Summaries are contained in F. S. Regs., Part II.
and the Staff Manual respectively. Title pages
will be prepared in manuscript.

Place	Date	Hour	Summary of Events and Information	Remarks and references to Appendices

Army Form C. 2118.

WAR DIARY
or
INTELLIGENCE SUMMARY.
(Erase heading not required.)

Instructions regarding War Diaries and Intelligence Summaries are contained in F. S. Regs., Part II. and the Staff Manual respectively. Title pages will be prepared in manuscript.

Place	Date	Hour	Summary of Events and Information	Remarks and references to Appendices
NIEURLET OUDEZEELE	1/5/18		Battalion marched in Brigade column to RYWELD AREA and camped at OUDEZEELE.	REF: MAP HAZEBROUCK No. 5A.
NIEURLET	2/5/18		Commanding Officer and Adjutant reconnoitred WATOU LINE. Battalion marched in Brigade column to NIEURLET. Captain G. E. Deacon rejoined Battalion from 3rd Echelon.	R.A.
	3/5/18		Companies under Company Commanders. Morning spent cleaning equipment. Afternoon - Lewis Gun Training.	R.A.
	4/5/18		Parades under Company Commanders. Major-General J. Ponsonby, C.B., C.M.G., D.S.O., presented Military Medal ribbands to N.C.Os and men of 119th Infantry Brigade (11008 Sgt. Waken T., 12407 Private Balcombe, W., and 7541 Private Gardner, W., of this Battalion) and addressed all ranks proceeding to the Base.	R.
	5/5/18		1 Officer and 447 O.Rs entrained at WATTEN for CALAIS. Lieut. R.F.McAloom, M.O.R.C. rejoined 136th Field Ambulance. Lieut. Col. H. L. Warden, D.S.O., proceeded on leave to ENGLAND. Captain F. S. Beecroft took over command of Battalion.	R.A.
	6/5/18		Battalion Training Staff moved to billets in BOONINGHEM.	R.A.
BOONINGHEM	7/5/18		Battalion transport inspected by General Vaughan, Inspector of Horsemanship to G.H.Q.	R.A.

WAR DIARY
or
INTELLIGENCE SUMMARY.

(Erase heading not required.)

Army Form C. 2118.

Place	Date	Hour	Summary of Events and Information	Remarks and references to Appendices
BOESINGHEM	8/5/18		Baths at ST. MOMELIN were allotted to the Battalion. Kit Inspection by the Adjutant in the afternoon.	hh
	9/5/18		Classes of Instruction under Senior Instructors carried out. Lecture by Commanding Officer.	nn
	10/5/18		Battalion Training Staff marched to STAPLE area via LEDERZEELE and L'HEY and camped in field in QUEUE D'OXELAERE.	kn
QUEUE D'OXELAERE	11/5/18		Battalion Training Staff deputed to suggest billets for a Division in Reserve. HONDEGHEM - TERDEGHEM area ('B' Section).	Jen
	12/5/18		Whole area reconnoitred by all Officers of Battalion Training Staff.	mn
	13/5/18		Positions fixed for suggested Brigade H.Q. and dumps. Commanding Officer attended conference at Brigade Headquarters.	Rl
	14/5/18		Billets for all units within a Division reconnoitred and fixed. Roads and tracks within the area useful for the evacuation of wounded, labour, and civilians, reconnoitred.	Nu
	15/5/18		Specialist Classes under Senior Instructors. Route march under the Orderly Officer in the afternoon.	Ro

WAR DIARY
or
INTELLIGENCE SUMMARY.

(Erase heading not required.)

Army Form C. 2118.

Place	Date	Hour	Summary of Events and Information	Remarks and references to Appendices
QUEUE D'OXELAERE	16/5/18		Specialist Classes under Senior Instructors. Route March under the Orderly Officer in the afternoon. The following Decorations were authorised:-	
			T/Lieut. (A/Capt.) F.S. BEECROFT. The Military Cross.	
			T/Lieut. J.E.M. CROWTHER. - do -	
			Lieut. H.W. Allason. - do -	
			T/2nd Lieut. G. R. TARRY. - do -	
			T/Capt. F. S. Ainger. - do -	
			T/Lieut. D. BERNEY, M.O.R.C., U.S.A. - do -	
			No. 482 C.S.M. R. REED. - do -	
			No. 11316 Pte. W. WARMAN. The Distinguished Conduct Medal	
			No. 24625 " J. GEARY. - do -	
			No. 13277 " F. EYLES. - do -	
			No. 8514 R.S.M. J. A. LEE. - do -	
			BAR TO THE DISTINGUISHED SERVICE ORDER.	
			T/Lieut. Col. H. L. WARDEN, D.S.O..	
	17/5/18		HONDEGHEM and TERDEGHEM SWITCHES reconnoitred.	
	18/5/18		Battalion Training Staff marched via WALLON CAPPEL to Camp at LA BELLE HOTESSE and deputed to suggest positions for a Division in the line in the LA BELLE HOTESSE - STEENBECQUE area. ('A' Section).	
LA BELLE HOTESSE			Suggested Out-post line in front of STEENBECQUE - LA BELLE HOTESSE Line reconnoitred.	

WAR DIARY
or
INTELLIGENCE SUMMARY.

(Erase heading not required.)

Army Form C. 2118.

Place	Date	Hour	Summary of Events and Information	Remarks and references to Appendices
LA BELLE HOTESSE	20/5/18		Suggested Brigade and Battalion H. Qrs., fixed.	
	21/5/18		Roads, tracks, and billets reconnoitred.	
	22/5/18		Whole area reconnoitred in conjunction with Lieut. Colonel Commanding "A" Section	
	23/5/18		Lieut. Col. H.L. Warden, D.S.O., returned from leave, and took over command of "A" Section, 40th Division.	
	24/5/18		Positions for suggested Brigade and Battalion Observation Posts reconnoitred.	
	25/5/18		Positions for suggested Divisional O.Ps reconnoitred.	
	26/5/18		Specialist Classes under Senior Instructors.	
	27/5/18		Specialist Classes under Senior Instructors.	
	28/5/18		Specialist Classes under Senior Instructors.	
	29/5/18		Specialist Classes under Senior Instructors. The Military Cross was granted to the following Officers of the Battalion:- T/Lieut. F. N. CORBEN. 2/Lieut. C. F. WILKS. T/2nd Lieut. W.T.H.SEWELL. T/Lieut. (a/Capt) H.S. DAINTREE.	

WAR DIARY
or
INTELLIGENCE SUMMARY.
(Erase heading not required.)

Army Form C. 2118.

Place	Date	Hour	Summary of Events and Information	Remarks and references to Appendices
LES TROIS ROIS	31/5/18			
	31/5/18		Battalion Training Staff moved to Camp near LES TROIS ROIS. Lieut. Col. H. L. Warden, D.S.O., returned from Commanding "A" Section, 40th Division, and resumed command of the Battalion. Specialist Classes under Senior Instructors.	

H. L. Warden, Lieut. Col.
Cmdg. 13th Bn. East Surrey Regt.

CONFIDENTIAL.

13TH (S) BN "EAST SURREY" REGT.

WAR DIARY

VOLUME No.

JUNE - 1918.

Army Form C. 2118.

WAR DIARY
or
INTELLIGENCE SUMMARY.
(Erase heading not required.)

Instructions regarding War Diaries and Intelligence Summaries are contained in F. S. Regs., Part II. and the Staff Manual respectively. Title pages will be prepared in manuscript.

Place	Date	Hour	Summary of Events and Information	Remarks and references to Appendices

Army Form C. 2118.

WAR DIARY
or
INTELLIGENCE SUMMARY.
(Erase heading not required.)

Instructions regarding War Diaries and Intelligence Summaries are contained in F. S. Regs., Part II. and the Staff Manual respectively. Title pages will be prepared in manuscript.

Place	Date	Hour	Summary of Events and Information	Remarks and references to Appendices
LES TROIS ARBRES	1/6/18		Training under Specialist Instructors.	MAREEBROUCK 5A
"	2/6/18		Training under Specialist Instructors.	
HARDINGHEM	3/6/18		Battalion Training Staff entrained at ARNEKE and detrained at RINXENT, then marched to HARDINGHEM, and was transferred to 102nd Infantry Brigade, 34th Division.	CASUALTIES SHEET 13A
	4/6/18		Training Staff engaged in finding billets for American Battalions in the HARDINGHEM AREA.	
	5/6/18		Billeting continued.	
	6/6/18		- do -	
	7/6/18		- do -	
	8/6/18		- do -	
	9/6/18		- do -	
	10/6/18		- do -	
BAYENGHEM	11/6/18		Battalion Training Staff marched to billets in BAYENGHEM, and was transferred to the 101st Infantry Brigade.	HAZEBROUCK 5A
	12/6/18		Battalion Training Staff engaged in finding billets for the 310th American Regiment.	

Army Form C. 2118.

WAR DIARY
or
INTELLIGENCE SUMMARY.
(Erase heading not required.)

Instructions regarding War Diaries and Intelligence Summaries are contained in F. S. Regs., Part II. and the Staff Manual respectively. Title pages will be prepared in manuscript.

Place	Date	Hour	Summary of Events and Information	Remarks and references to Appendices
BAYENGHEM	13/6/18		1st Battalion, 310th American Regiment, moved into billets in WATTERDAL: 3rd Battalion, moved into billets in BAYENGHEM. Battalion Training Cadre affiliated to 1st and 3rd Battalions, 310th American Regiment. Lieut. Col. H.L. Warden, D.S.O., took over command of the 310th Regimental School at SENINGHEM.	Appendix 1
	14/6/18		Training in progress.	
	15/6/18		- do -	
	16/6/18		- do -	
	17/6/18		Commander-in-Chief of the British Forces in France. 310th American Regiment inspected by the	
	18/6/18		Training in progress.	
	19/6/18		- do -	
	20/6/18		- do -	
	21/6/18		- do -	
	22/6/18		- do -	
	23/6/18		- do -	
	24/6/18		- do -	
	25/6/18		- do -	
	26/6/18		- do -	

Army Form C. 2118.

WAR DIARY
or
INTELLIGENCE SUMMARY.
(Erase heading not required.)

Instructions regarding War Diaries and Intelligence Summaries are contained in F. S. Regs., Part II. and the Staff Manual respectively. Title pages will be prepared in manuscript.

Place	Date	Hour	Summary of Events and Information	Remarks and references to Appendices
BAYENGHEM	27/6/19		Battalion Training Staff warned to be in readiness to proceed to England to be reconstituted with the 25th Division.	
	28/6/19		Training in progress.	
	29/6/19		Battalion Training Staff proceeded to BOULOGNE en route for ENGLAND to be reconstituted with the 25th Division.	
	30/6/19		Battalion Training Staff proceeded to ENGLAND.	

H. J. Sanders
Lieut. Colonel,
Commanding 13th (Ser.) Batt. E. Surrey Regt.

26D

13TH (S) BN EAST SURREY REGT.

WAR DIARY
VOLUME No.
JULY - 1918

WAR DIARY
or
INTELLIGENCE SUMMARY.

(Erase heading not required.)

Army Form C. 2118.

Place	Date	Hour	Summary of Events and Information	Remarks and references to Appendices
MYTCHETT CAMP ALDERSHOT	1/7/17		The Battalion Training Staff proceeded to England yesterday, 30th June, and arrived at ALDERSHOT in the evening. (9 Officers and 47 Other Ranks) It was accommodated in U.S.A. Camp, Mytchett, nr. Frimley, Aldershot, together with the Division. Brigade, and other Battalion training staffs of the 25th Division. The Battalion Training Staff was informed that the men required to form the Battalion were not yet available. Meanwhile the Training Staff was posted to the 7th Infantry Brigade (Brigadier General C. R. Hickie) together with the 8th Bn. Leicester Regt and 10th Bn. Cheshire Regt. afterwards changed to the 14th West Riding Regt. and the 15th Bn. South Wales Borderers respectively.	
"	2/7/17		Still awaiting orders. 50% of the Training Staff was granted 7 days leave. Lieut. F.N.Corben, M.C. proceeded to Aldershot Command Musketry School to attend Lewis Gun Course.	
"	3/7/17		Still awaiting orders.	
"	4/7/17		Awaiting orders.	
"	5/7/17		Awaiting orders. Lieut. Col. H.L. Warden, D.S.O. proceeded on 7 days leave, together with 30% of the Training Staff.	
"	6/7/17		Awaiting orders.	
"	7/7/17		Awaiting orders.	
"	8/7/17		Awaiting orders. 50% of the Training Staff returned from leave.	
"	9/7/17		Awaiting orders. Remainder of the Training Staff proceeded on 7 days leave. A/Capt. W.T.H.Sewell, M.C. Proceeded to Aldershot Command Bombing School.	

Army Form C. 2118.

WAR DIARY
or
INTELLIGENCE SUMMARY.
(Erase heading not required.)

Instructions regarding War Diaries and Intelligence Summaries are contained in F. S. Regs., Part II. and the Staff Manual respectively. Title pages will be prepared in manuscript.

Place	Date	Hour	Summary of Events and Information	Remarks and references to Appendices
ALDERSHOT	1/4/18		Awaiting orders. Rifle inspection parades only.	
"	2/4/18		Awaiting orders. Rifle inspection parades only. 30% of the Training Staff who proceeded on leave on the 5th inst., returned.	
"	3/4/18		The G.O.C., 7th Infantry Brigade, inspected the Training Cadre in the vicinity of their lines at 10.30 a.m.	
"	4/4/18		Awaiting orders. Lieut. D.O.Macdonald (R.A.M.C.) reported to this unit for duty.	
"	5/4/18		Awaiting orders. Instructions received for the Training Staff to proceed to LOWESTOFT on the 16th inst., for the purpose of collecting the men and re-forming this Battalion.	
"	15/4/18		Rifle inspections and preparations for the move. Remainder of the Training Staff returned from leave.	
"	16/4/18		The Battalion Training Staff moved by train to LOWESTOFT via WATERLOO and LIVERPOOL STREET STATIONS arriving at LOWESTOFT at about 9.30 p.m. The Training Cadre was met at the Station by the undermentioned Officers who were to be attached to assist in re-forming the Battalion. Accommodation was provided at the Empire Hotel, LOWESTOFT. Major W.H.B.Whitaker (2/1 Montgomery Yeomanry), Capt. A.Rowbotham (2/25 London Regt), Capt. H.S.Okeover (6th Bn. Middlesex Regt), 2/Lieut. E. H. Davies (6th Bn. Middlesex Regt), Lieut. A.Palmer (2/1 Dnbh. Yeomanry), 2/Lieut. H. L. Bach (2/1 Montgomery Yeomanry).	

WAR DIARY
or
INTELLIGENCE SUMMARY.

(Erase heading not required.)

Army Form C. 2118.

Place	Date	Hour	Summary of Events and Information	Remarks and references to Appendices
WESTOFT	19/1/17		The whole of the Training Staff established at the Empire Hotel, LOWESTOFT, in readiness to receive drafts. Training Cadre now under the administration of the 225th Mixed Brigade, ST. OLAVES. (58th Welsh Division) A draft of 74 O.Rs (11 from 5th Bn. East Surrey Regt. Crowborough, and 63 from the 3rd Bn. East Surrey Regt, Dover) which had arrived at LOWESTOFT before the Training Cadre, was paraded in the grounds of the Hotel in the morning and posted to Companies. The Other Ranks of the Training Cadre were also posted to Companies. The Company Commanders at this stage were:- "A" Coy. Capt. E. E. Dodd. "B" " A/Capt. C.P.Wilks, M.C. "C" " A/Capt. V.T.H.Sewell, M.C. "D" " Capt. F. S. Beecroft, M.C.	R
"	2/1/18		Companies at disposal of Os. C. Coys.	R
"	3/1/18		Companies at disposal of Os. C. Coys. Preparations in progress for the accommodation of future drafts.	R
"	4/1/18		Companies at the disposal of Os. C. Coys. Drafts arrived to-day as follows:- 3 O.Rs. Cat. B.i. from 5th Bn.E.Surrey.Regt. Crowborough. 34 O.Rs. " B.ii " 3rd - do - Dover.	R
"	5/1/18		Companies at the disposal of Os. C. Companies. Lieut. F.R.Woodward appointed temporarily as Messing Officer as from to-day's date.	R

WAR DIARY
or
INTELLIGENCE SUMMARY.

Army Form C. 2118.

Place	Date	Hour	Summary of Events and Information	Remarks and references to Appendices
LOWESTOFT	22/11		Issuing of rifles and equipment to all men as far as possible. Battalion Ceremonial Parade in the grounds of the Hotel at 10 a.m. For the remainder of the day, Companies at disposal of Os. C. Coys. Drafts arrived to-day as follows:- 7 O.Rs. B.i. from 4th Bn. East Surrey Regt., Felixstowe. 3 " B.ii " 11th Bn. Bedfordshire Regt., Lowestoft.	
	23/11		9 to 9.30 a.m. Battalion Ceremonial Parade. Remainder of the day devoted to the cleaning up of equipment, rifles, etc., and bayonet inspections by Company Commanders. During the afternoon the Corps Commander inspected the Battalion at its training which consisted of Specialist Classes, namely: Musketry, Lewis Gun, Bombing, and Scouting. Drafts arrived to-day as follows:- 14 O.Rs (13 B.i.) from 3rd Bn. East Surrey Regt. Dover. 1 B.ii)	
	24/11		9 to 9.30 a.m. Ceremonial. 9.30 to 12.30. Companies at the disposal of Company Commanders. Remainder of the day's parade hours devoted to Specialist Classes. Drafts arrived to-day as follows:- 7 O.Rs. B.ii from 4th Bn. E.Surrey Regt. Felixstowe. 6 " B.ii " 3rd Bn. Suffolk Regt. " 7 " B.ii " 3rd Bn. Norfolk Regt. " 59 " B.ii " 3rd Bn. Essex 31st. " 24 " B.ii " 3rd Bn. Bedfordshire Regt. "	
	25/11		Battalion Ceremonial Parade. Rifle inspection by Musketry Sergeant. Specialist Classes.	
	26/11		Companies at the disposal of Os. C. Companies.	

Army Form C. 2118.

WAR DIARY
or
INTELLIGENCE SUMMARY.
(Erase heading not required.)

Instructions regarding War Diaries and Intelligence Summaries are contained in F. S. Regs., Part II. and the Staff Manual respectively. Title pages will be prepared in manuscript.

Place	Date	Hour	Summary of Events and Information	Remarks references to Appendices
LOWESTOFT	1/4/17		9. to 10.30 a.m. Battalion Ceremonial Parade on the Lowestoft Golf Links. 10.30 - 11.30 a.m. Extended Order Drill by Companies. 11.30 - 12.30 p.m. Musketry exercises. The afternoon was a half-holiday.	
"	2/4/17		Companies at the disposal of Os. C. Companies.	
"	3/4/17		Battalion Ceremonial Parade. Extended Order Drill by Companies and Platoons. Musketry exercises. Specialist Classes. Drafts arrived to-day as follows:- 9 O.Rs. B.i. from 21st London Regt. Wrentham.	
"	4/4/17		Ceremonial and Battalion drill. Extended Order drill. Musketry exercises. Specialist Classes. The ground for all training has now been established on Lowestoft Golf Links. Draft arrived to-day as follows:- 10 O.Rs. B.i. from 3rd Bn. East Surrey Regt, Dover.	
"	5/4/17		Inspection by the 25th Divisional Commander (Major General Sir David Bainbridge) in the grounds of the Hotel from 11 a.m. to 12.30 p.m. For the remainder of the day parades as usual. Drafts received to-day as follows:- 12 O.Rs B.i. from 3rd Bn. Suffolk Regt. Felixstowe. 20 " A & B.i. " 4th Bn. E.Surrey Regt. " 91 " B.ii " 5th Royal Fusiliers, Dover. x 6 " - " 19th Queens (R.W.S.) Regt, Lowestoft. x These men proceeded direct to Colchester as part of the personnel for 7th Light Trench Mortar Battery.	

Army Form C. 2118.

WAR DIARY
or
INTELLIGENCE SUMMARY.
(Erase heading not required.)

Instructions regarding War Diaries and Intelligence Summaries are contained in F. S. Regs., Part II. and the Staff Manual respectively. Title pages will be prepared in manuscript.

Summary of Events and Information

Place	Date	Hour		Remarks and references to Appendices
LOWESTOFT	30/6/18		The names and appointments of the Officers who proceeded to IRELAND with the Training Staff on the 30th June, 1918, are as follows:—	
			Lieut. Col. H.L. Wright. D.S.O. — Commanding Officer	
			Capt. G. E. Deacon. — Adjutant	
			Capt. F. G. Beacon. — Company Commander	
			A/Capt. C. F. Wilkes.	
			A/Capt. V. E. Samuell.	
			Capt. E. E. Dunn.	
			Lieut. F. E. Coleman.	
			Lieut. F. L. Woolard.	
			Lieut. & Q.M. J. _____	

www.ingramcontent.com/pod-product-compliance
Lightning Source LLC
Chambersburg PA
CBHW081244170426
43191CB00034B/2041